D0894390

DATE DUE

12/16/13	
4/15/14	
4/16/14	
9/22/14	

DEMCO, INC. 38-2931

THE TRUTH ABOUT
METHAMPHETAMINE
AND
CRYSTAL METH

LARA NORQUIST and FRANK SPALDING

ROSEN
PUBLISHING

New York

Published in 2012 by The Rosen Publishing Group, Inc.
29 East 21st Street, New York, NY 10010

Copyright © 2012 by The Rosen Publishing Group, Inc.

First Edition

Library of Congress Cataloging-in-Publication Data

Norquist, Lara.
The truth about methamphetamine and crystal meth/Lara Norquist, Frank Spalding.—1st ed.
    p. cm.—(Drugs & consequences)
Includes bibliographical references and index.
ISBN 978-1-4488-4641-2 (library binding)
1. Methamphetamine abuse—Juvenile literature. 2. Methamphetamine—Juvenile literature. 3. Ice (Drug)—Juvenile literature. 4. Teenagers—Drug use—Juvenile literature. I. Spalding, Frank. II. Title.
RC568.A45N67 2012
362.29'9—dc22
                                                                2010049958

Manufactured in the United States of America

CPSIA Compliance Information: Batch #S11YA: For further information, contact Rosen Publishing, New York, New York, at 1-800-237-9932.

CONTENTS

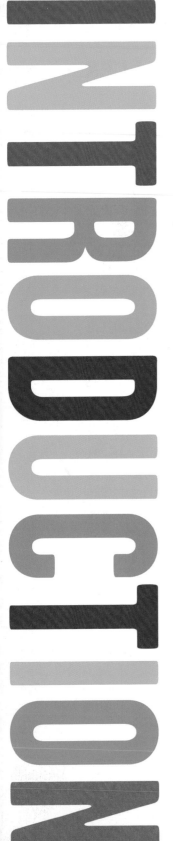
INTRODUCTION

Methamphetamine is a stimulant, or a drug that increases the activity of the body's nervous system. Stimulants act on a person's central nervous system, making a user feel more energetic, alert, and productive. Some stimulants, such as caffeine, are perfectly legal. Other stimulants, such as cocaine, crack, ecstasy, and methamphetamine, are illegal. Methamphetamine, commonly known as meth, comes in granular or powder form. It can also be manufactured in chunks known as crystal meth (and also referred to as "ice" or "glass"). Meth is one of the most popular illicit drugs in the United States. It is simple to make, profitable for dealers, and highly addictive.

Methamphetamine is the most commonly abused type of amphetamine. It is a powerful synthetic (human-made) psychostimulant drug. People use meth to increase alertness and decisiveness, relieve fatigue, and feel stronger. Consequences of methamphetamine use can include rapid addiction, psychotic behavior, and brain damage. Long-term, habitual use can cause violent behavior, anxiety, confusion, insomnia, auditory hallucinations, mood disturbances, delusions, and paranoia. Withdrawal symptoms include depression, anxiety, fatigue, paranoia, and intense cravings.

Meth use can damage the body's organs, including the heart, leading to heart failure, strokes, and convulsions. It can also alter and damage your brain chemistry, resulting in long-term depression and anxiety.

Meth is now considered to be one of the most dangerous drugs in the United States. At one time, it was considered a drug that mainly appealed to low-income white men living in rural areas. Although meth is still popular with this group, today all sorts of people use methamphetamine. As a result, the dangers of meth are increasing, and the damage being wreaked is more widespread. The costs to taxpayers of enforcing meth laws, funding law enforcement raids of meth labs, and shouldering the court and jail expenses of those caught up in drug-related crimes are spiraling ever upward. More important the social costs of meth manufacturing, distribution, and use—from environmental degradation to the disintegration of families—are fraying the very fabric of American society. Meth is a toxic drug that seeks to kill everything it comes into contact with, including the user, his or her family, and the community at large.

CHAPTER 1

HOW METH EMERGED

Methamphetamine is chemically similar to a drug called amphetamine, which was first synthesized in Germany in 1887. In the 1920s, researchers experimented with using amphetamine to treat a number of diseases, such as epilepsy, schizophrenia, and alcoholism. The drug was also suggested as a treatment for depression. By 1927, scientists and doctors had discovered that amphetamine raised patients' blood pressure and enlarged their nasal passages. It also enlarged their bronchial passages, the tubes that carry air in and out of the lungs when a person breathes.

A variation of amphetamine was first commercially released as a decongestant under the name Benzedrine in 1928. Benzedrine could be purchased at most local pharmacies with a prescription. The drug came in inhalers similar to the kind used by asthmatics. Many people who used Benzedrine discovered that the drug had a mild euphoric effect. It wasn't long before people hit upon the idea of breaking open the inhaler to consume the drug all at once instead of in small doses. Inside the inhaler, a small strip of paper soaked in the drug could be removed and swallowed. Slowly but surely, Benzedrine gained in popularity among drug abusers. By the time reports emerged about the spread of Benzedrine inhaler misuse, thousands of people all over the country were using the drug.

By the late 1930s, amphetamine was being manufactured in pill form, further increasing the availability of the drug. This form of amphetamine was intended to combat narcolepsy, a disease in which sufferers fall asleep at unpredictable times and without warning.

Methamphetamine, which is a chemical related to amphetamine, was first synthesized by a Japanese chemist in 1919. It had a very similar effect to amphetamine, with two important distinctions: methamphetamine was much more potent and much cheaper to make. It didn't become widely available until 1942, when the Second World War was under way.

Coming Home Addicted

Many American servicemen returned from fighting in World War II and, later, from the Korean War (1950–1953) with a desire to get more methamphetamine. It was still possible to buy Benzedrine and other types of amphetamine and methamphetamine with a prescription, but soon these supplies and dosages weren't enough to keep up with the demand of addicts. Whatever the intended medical uses of amphetamine and methamphetamine, it was clear that more and more people were acquiring them for recreational use.

By the 1950s, doctors had grown concerned about excessively prescribing Benzedrine to their patients. In response to this spreading stimulant abuse in the United States, the U.S. Drug Abuse Regulation and Control Act of 1970 made amphetamine illegal.

Meth: A Soldier's Friend

During World War II (1939–1945), methamphetamine was distributed to soldiers on both sides of the conflict. Pilots often took to the air with a supply of methamphetamine to help them stay alert during long missions. The Axis powers of Germany and Japan gave methamphetamine to their soldiers to help them stay awake, alert, and energized in combat. Methamphetamine allowed soldiers to perform better with less rest than they could otherwise. Many soldiers fighting for the

Many World War II–era pilots and other servicemen on both sides of the conflict were provided with methamphetamine before combat operations. Pilots used the drug in order to stay awake and alert during long-distance nighttime bombing raids.

Allied powers, such as Great Britain, Canada, and the United States, also used methamphetamine on the battlefield.

By the time the Axis powers surrendered in 1945, World War II had spread tremendous destruction across the world. Millions of people had lost their lives, and many cities had been reduced to rubble. Some countries took a long time to rebuild completely. Amid all this ruin and chaos, almost no one noticed that in Japan, meth addiction was spreading throughout the population.

One of the conditions of Japan's surrender after World War II was that it dismantle its military. Without a standing military, Japan no longer had a need for methamphetamine, and the drug was immediately banned. However, there was still a lot of methamphetamine in storage. Many of the Japanese and Allied soldiers who had grown accustomed to using it did not want to stop now that the war was over. Organized crime syndicates realized that these addicts presented a huge potential customer base. Even though the drug was banned, it became widely available on the black market.

An Ongoing Problem

A recent survey conducted of county law enforcement officials around the United States shows that meth is considered the number-one drug problem today, ahead of even cocaine and marijuana. The National Association of Counties (NACO) conducted a survey of law enforcement officials from forty-five states. The survey results showed that 47 percent of county sheriffs felt that meth was their greatest drug problem. Only 21 percent felt cocaine was, while 22 percent believed marijuana posed the greatest local threat. The U.S. Department of Justice's most recent National Drug Threat Assessment Report echoed these findings, reporting that 68 percent of state and local agencies in the twenty western states consider meth to be their greatest drug threat. Only 19 percent of these agencies felt cocaine was the greatest threat. The criminal justice costs of

A surprise raid on a meth superlab is conducted by officers of the Fresno, California, Meth Task Force.

enforcing meth laws has soared to over $4 billion a year, and 55 percent of county sheriffs report rising rates of robberies and burglaries associated with meth use and trade. The total cost of meth use to society is estimated to be more than $23 billion a year, including the costs associated with court proceedings, imprisonment, drug treatment and rehabilitation services, health care, and foster care. So not only does the drug hurt users, it wreaks havoc upon communities and families and siphons local and national law-enforcement money, both in preventive and cleanup measures.

2

WHEN METH TAKES OVER

M any of the first people who became addicted to methamphetamine and amphetamine were taking the medications for other purposes, such as to stay awake or control their diet. Today, some people still use meth to generate energy and wakefulness for commonplace tasks. For example, they might use meth before a long shift at work or during an all-night study session. According to Quest Diagnostics, a company that performs drug

Many meth users take the drug in order to stay awake and stimulated during extended periods of work. They are unprepared, however, for the debilitating crash that follows and can last for days.

tests for employers and businesses, the number of employees who tested positive for methamphetamine in the United States rose steadily in the first decade of the twenty-first century. The percentage of employees testing positive for amphetamine more than doubled since 2000, to the point where one in every two hundred employees tested positive for the drug. Ten percent of all positive results from workplace drug tests involved the presence of amphetamine.

The Health and Human Services 2009 National Survey on Drug Use and Health found that the number of recent new users of methamphetamine among persons aged 12 or older was 154,000 in 2009. This estimate was significantly higher than the estimate for 2008 (95,000). It also found that the average age of new methamphetamine users aged 12 to 49 in 2009 was 19.3 years. More than 10 million Americans aged 12 or older have tried meth at least once in their lives, representing more than 4 percent of the 12 and older population. Almost 3 percent of eighth graders report having used meth at least once. More than one million Americans use meth each year, and about half a million use it in any given month. The number of meth-dependent users is close to 300,000 nationwide, a more than 10 percent increase since 2005.

The Slippery Slope of Addiction

When people first use meth, they usually don't think that they're going to end up a meth addict. People often start using meth recreationally at parties and social gatherings. Before long, they begin using it alone. As time passes, they find that they are unable to stop. Many users start using meth by snorting it. They then progress to smoking it and then to injecting it directly into their veins. Methamphetamine is so addictive that it can become more important than the user's job, friends, and loved ones. It can destroy the user's professional, social, and family life, and finally destroy the mind and body.

Not Taking Care of Business

Many people who are under the influence of meth during school or work just think that they're being productive, which is why the drug is becoming more popular among college students and in competitive and stressful professional fields. For instance, the California Bar Association has reported that one in four lawyers who seek treatment for drug addiction is a habitual meth user. Even though these meth users may have what appear to be normal lives, they are still harming themselves.

When people turn to meth to help them meet their deadlines and work long hours, they push their bodies to the limits of their endurance. However, meth isn't a relatively harmless drug like caffeine. While it may increase wakefulness, too much meth will disrupt the central nervous system, making it difficult for a user to think clearly. Students who use meth or other illegal stimulants in an effort to finish writing term papers may complete their assignment, only to find the next day that their work is nonsensical. In some industries, such as construction or farming, this disorientation can lead to workplace accidents, serious injuries, and even death.

The Dangerous Side Effects of Meth

Meth can be swallowed, snorted, smoked, or injected directly into a user's veins. A person using meth feels euphoria, or

Rave and club culture helped boost the popularity of meth. It remains a popular though deadly party drug. Yet the energy rush and euphoria partiers seek can end in dangerous dehydration, dizziness, convulsions, strokes, heart attacks, and even death.

intense pleasure, soon after taking it. This is called a rush or flash. This rush generally occurs within just five to twenty minutes and gradually fades away. The post-rush effects of the drug can last for a very long time, sometimes as long as twelve hours. During this time, the user's body temperature rises, the heart rate increases, and the appetite decreases.

Meth's most significant effect, however, is the extreme amount of energy and wakefulness that the user experiences.

The intense high is one of the main reasons meth users like taking the drug so much. It is also one of the reasons people can become addicted to meth so quickly. Few other drugs have such an intense and long-lasting effect on users. Then again, few drugs cause as much harm to their users as meth does.

All illicit drugs take a toll on those who use them, but meth is especially damaging. Once meth's initial rush wears off, the user often feels deep depression, coupled with an intense desire to consume more of the drug. Some meth users go into violent rages, making them dangerous to themselves and others. Chronic long-term use of methamphetamine can result in paranoia, hallucinations, convulsions, heart attack, brain damage, stroke, and eventually death. Even if meth users are aware that they are becoming addicts, they are often powerless to stop their downward spiral.

From Rush and Tweaking to Crash and Addiction

Lasting only a few minutes, the initial rush often becomes more and more elusive for meth users as their bodies build up tolerance to the drug. Users sometimes find themselves using meth over an entire weekend, staying awake the whole time and trying to relive that initial rush. The longer the meth user stays awake, the more out of control he or she becomes, often growing confused, irritable, and extremely paranoid. Some users begin to have minor hallucinations.

This hard-hitting billboard, part of the Montana Meth Project, highlights one of the grotesque side effects of meth use: "crank bugs." This is the sensation or hallucination that bugs are crawling on or under a user's skin.

Repeatedly using meth can keep a user from sleeping for well over a week. Users often keep taking more and more meth to try and stay awake, but they are unable to recapture the euphoric effects of the first hit. This stage of meth use is known as tweaking. While tweaking, the user is likely to engage in simple, repetitive tasks. These tasks can include taking something apart and then putting it back together again, or repeatedly cleaning his or her room. It's not uncommon for meth users to pick at the skin of their arms and face while tweaking or hallucinate that there are insects (sometimes referred to as "crank bugs") underneath their skin. At this point, their judgment is severely impaired, and there is an increased chance that they may harm themselves or others.

Even though chronic meth users can stay awake for days at a time, no one can stay awake forever. Eventually, users will give in to fatigue and depression. After staying awake for several days, meth users will crash, their bodies and brains completely exhausted. Users may sleep for several days straight following a meth binge.

CHAPTER 3

THE ROAD TO ADDICTION

A person is considered an addict if she or he keeps using a drug even though she or he knows it is harmful. An addict may also be physically dependent on the drug. Physical dependence is when the body craves more of the drug and is unable to function normally without it. Addicts deprived of the substances they are dependent upon go through withdrawal, which can often be physically and mentally harrowing.

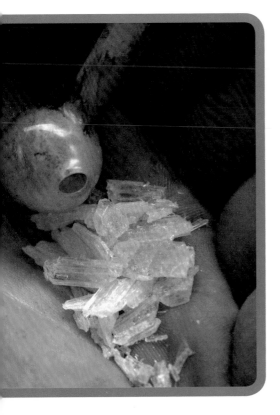

The crystal form of methamphetamine—crystal meth—is smoked in a glass pipe like the one that appears here. Sharing pipes, just like sharing needles, spreads potentially deadly infections.

Addiction Theories

A user's risk of addiction depends on many physical and psychological factors, including personality, social environment, and peer influences. Some people have brain chemistries that make them more inclined to addiction, and some people are psychologically predisposed to addiction. It's impossible to tell which casual meth users may one day become meth addicts.

No one is quite sure what causes addiction, but there are a number of theories as to why some people seem to be more susceptible to addiction than others. These theories are often called models.

Moral "Deficiency"

According to the moral model of addiction, drug dependence is the result of something wrong in the addict's character. People who believe in this model of addiction think that there are no biological causes for drug addiction and that the only reason that an addict keeps abusing substances is that the addict doesn't really want to quit. While it might be comforting for some people to believe that all drug addicts are just weak people who should know better, this model of addiction does not hold much weight in the scientific community.

Genetic Predisposition

According to the genetic model of addiction, certain biological factors can help predict who might be at risk of becoming drug dependent. For instance, a history of substance abuse in a person's family may be an indicator that that person is vulnerable to addiction. While many experts cite compelling evidence that people can inherit a genetic predisposition to addiction, many

An American Problem

About 3.5–5.7 percent of the world's population aged 15 to 64 consumed illicit drugs in the previous year, according to the United Nations 2010 World Drug Report. Approximately 2.8 percent of the U.S. population aged 12 or older—7 million people—are substance dependent and abuse drugs. Studies have shown that addiction generally affects young people the most, as well as people on the lower end of the socioeconomic spectrum. This doesn't mean, however, that there aren't plenty of people in the middle and upper classes who don't also suffer from substance abuse and addiction.

professionals believe that family environment also plays an important role. People born into a family of substance abusers may be more likely to abuse substances themselves—whether or not they are genetically predisposed to addiction. Many scientists believe that a combination of genetics and learned behavior makes some people more likely to become addicts.

Addiction as Disease

According to the disease model of addiction, chemical dependency is an illness, much like diabetes and heart disease. Addiction, like a disease, can be acute, chronic, or progressive. The disease model states that there is no cure to addiction, but treating it through abstinence is the best way to control the addiction. Under this model, addicts must abstain from (completely refrain from using) substances for the rest of their lives if they hope to avoid relapsing into addiction.

4

THE DANGEROUS AND
DISGUSTING
SIDE EFFECTS OF
METH

Methamphetamine has profound effects on the body. It dries out the skin and causes rashes, extensive sweating, insomnia, and diarrhea. It affects the part of the brain that regulates heart rate, body temperature, appetite, and mood. When a user takes meth, the heart rate increases, the body temperature rises, and the mood temporarily improves before plummeting again with a post-euphoria crash. This can place a heavy strain on the body and, over time, can result in damage to the heart, lungs, and brain chemistry. Meth users may experience cardiac arrhythmia, or an irregular heartbeat. Taking too much of the drug can cause a user to suffer convulsions, heart attack, stroke, or death.

Greater Risk of Infections

One of the biggest risks meth users face is the chance that they will contract a disease from other users. Meth is often smoked out of glass pipes. Users sharing hot pipes run the risk of getting burns and sores to the lips, mouth, or gums. Bacterial and viral infections can easily be transmitted through these sores. Meth users face the danger of infection with human immunodeficiency virus (HIV; the virus that causes AIDS) and hepatitis C, both of which are contracted through blood-to-blood contact. Sharing straws in order to snort the drug also puts users at risk of infection by HIV and hepatitis C, a potentially fatal disease that attacks the liver and for which there is no cure. Sharing needles is the most dangerous way to take meth, as it allows for contact with other people's blood and other bodily fluids that can then enter the user's own bloodstream, greatly increasing the risk of infection and disease. Meth also lowers users' inhibitions, increases their sex drive, and impairs their judgment. This may encourage users to engage in unsafe sex, dramatically increasing their risk for contracting HIV and other sexually transmitted diseases.

Struggling with Withdrawal

Physical withdrawal from methamphetamine has less pronounced physical effects than those associated with other drugs, but the process can still be dangerous. Mentally,

"Meth Mouth": Tooth Decay

One very visible—and disgusting—effect of the drug is the damage it does to a user's teeth. Meth often causes people to grind their teeth. It also dries out users' mouths, and sometimes makes them crave sugary drinks. In addition, meth users typically neglect their dental hygiene, going for long periods without brushing or flossing. Meth itself is quite acidic and can wear the enamel off of teeth. "Meth mouth" is a term used to describe the excessive tooth decay from which heavy meth users tend to suffer.

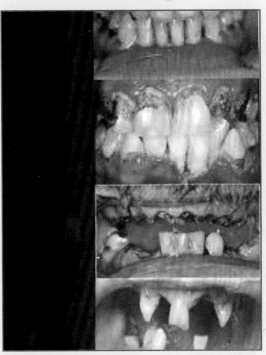

The ravages of "meth mouth" are displayed at a methamphetamine community awareness meeting.

methamphetamine addicts complain that they feel sluggish or mentally slow after giving up meth. The psychological component of meth addiction is very strong. Coupled with the low cost and wide availability of meth, it can be very difficult for an addict to stop using.

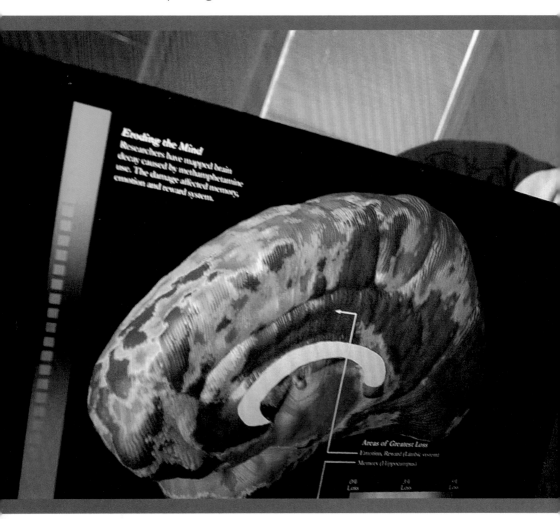

Dr. Jack Stump, a leading researcher on the effects of methamphetamine use, shows a PET scan of a meth user's brain and the damage the drug does.

Altering and Damaging Brain Chemistry

Methamphetamine alters the way the brain handles a chemical called dopamine, which is produced naturally by the body. Dopamine helps determine how the brain controls the move-

ments of the body and affects the way the brain processes information. A lack of dopamine can interfere with a person's memory and attention span. Parkinson's disease, which causes its victims to tremble uncontrollably, is a result of a shortage of dopamine in the brain. Disruption in the release of dopamine has been linked to severe mental illness.

Of all the important functions that dopamine performs, one of the most crucial is the way it provides the sensations of pleasure, enjoyment, satisfaction, and motivation. When dopamine is released, the brain is flooded with pleasurable feelings. This is part of the body's natural reward system. Dopamine is released when a person does healthy things like eat, exercise, or fall in love. Pleasure is a powerful motivator; unconsciously, we strive to do things that will cause our bodies to release more dopamine. In this sense, people are "addicted" to the things that will help them stay alive and lead a prosperous life.

Meth causes the body to release dopamine, but it also blocks the brain from reabsorbing it. The dopamine stays in the brain longer, resulting in a feeling of euphoria that is very hard to achieve naturally. This means that meth disrupts the body's natural reward system. There are few things a meth user could do that would flood the brain with as much dopamine as meth does. For this reason, the lives of users begin to center around the drug, and the addicts start neglecting things that were once important to them. Nothing can provide addicts with the same amount of pleasure as doing drugs. Hanging out with friends, listening to music, having a good meal, going out dancing, exercising, or even falling in love all pale in comparison to the synthetic rush of meth.

The body can release only a limited amount of dopamine. Although meth users may take more and more of the drug, they will be chemically unable to derive the same amount of pleasure from it that they first did. Studies show that long-term meth use may impact the ability of a user's brain to keep producing dopamine, and thus can cause brain damage. Some users undergo profound periods of depression and have suicidal thoughts once their brain chemistry has been altered.

MYTHS & FACTS

MYTH Using meth is a safe way to gain energy and lose weight.

FACT Because it increases metabolism and suppresses appetite, meth does cause weight loss, but this weight loss is extreme. Food gives people stamina in the form of calories that can be burned for energy. Meth, however, burns through the body's natural stores of energy. After that energy is gone, the user crashes, sometimes sleeping for days at a time. Meth use and abuse can result in heart and lung damage, cardiac arrhythmia (an irregular heartbeat), convulsions, heart attack, stroke, or death.

MYTH It's safe to use meth occasionally.

FACT Meth is extremely toxic, and any amount may damage the body. Even if a person uses meth only once, he or she could still overdose on the drug, suffer a heart attack, or have a stroke.

MYTH Meth mouth is caused by smoking the toxic, acidic chemicals used to manufacture methamphetamine and can be avoided by ingesting meth in a different way.

FACT Meth mouth is primarily caused by users grinding their teeth and the poor dental hygiene of many addicts. Also, meth causes the mouth to produce less saliva than normal, depriving users of the natural enzymes that help prevent tooth decay.

CHAPTER 5

DISABLING THE MACHINERY OF METH PRODUCTION

When powerful stimulants were restricted by the U.S. Drug Abuse Regulation and Control Act of 1970, drug dealers learned how to make meth in illegal laboratories. Even before then, the manufacture of meth was largely controlled by outlaw motorcycle gangs in the 1960s.

By the 1970s, cocaine became widely available. This made it the stimulant of choice among drug users, and methamphetamine became less common. Although it was not as widespread as before, meth did not disappear. By the 1980s, new ways to make meth were discovered that were fairly simple. Although yielding a much less pure form of the drug, manufacturing meth became easy and inexpensive. As the cost of the drug went down, its popularity began to rise once more.

Meth Production in Labs

Most of the meth found in the United States was being illegally manufactured in California by the 1980s. Although the West Coast is still the center of meth production in the United States, there are now meth labs all across the country. Unlike drugs that must be smuggled across the globe to reach North America, most of the meth available today is manufactured in clandestine local laboratories, or meth labs. Many of the ingredients used to create meth can be purchased over the counter at a drugstore. In 2009, more

A member of a hazmat team cleans up a meth lab raided in North Little Rock, Arkansas.

than 10,000 meth labs were seized in the United States. That's an average of 200 meth labs in each state.

Pure methamphetamine has no color. Meth produced in illegal laboratories may be white, yellow, or come in darker colors, depending on what chemicals were used to make it. Meth can come in a granulated powder or be formed into solid chunks. Meth is often called by a number of different names, such as speed, crank, or Tina. Meth that comes in solid chunks is often called crystal, ice, or glass. These forms of the drug are also smokable.

Meth labs come in all sizes. Larger meth labs, known as superlabs, can take up an entire building. Superlabs produce large amounts of meth for distribution throughout the country. To be classified as a superlab, the laboratory must produce more than 10 pounds (4.5 kilograms) of meth within twenty-four hours. About 80 percent of all meth in the United States is produced in superlabs.

Many meth labs are set up in private homes. People who invest a few hundred dollars in ingredients can make their own meth. Although the process for making meth is easy, it is very harmful for those making it and for those who inhabit the home laboratory. Meth is produced with toxic chemicals that stay on countertops, emit harmful fumes, and can cause long-term health dangers to those who are exposed to the chemicals. The fact that a good number of people who try to produce meth end up in jail, the hospital, or dead doesn't seem to deter would-be dealers.

The Toxic Ingredients of Meth

Meth is a dangerous drug, but manufacturing it can be even more dangerous. Recipes for making meth have changed over the years, depending on the cost and availability of the ingredients. One of the major ingredients in meth used to be a chemical called phenyl-2-propanone, which became a federally controlled substance in 1980.

After this chemical was banned, meth was generally made from ephedrine and pseudoephedrine. The meth cooks who resorted to using ephedrine found that it made the drug much more potent. Ephedrine and pseudoephedrine are primarily used in decongestants and can be found in many over-the-counter medicines.

The other chemicals used to make meth are acidic enough to eat through skin and bone. They can include chemicals found in drain cleaners and paint thinners, ammonia, and sulfuric acid. Many of these chemicals are so toxic that even being in a meth lab is dangerous. Some meth cooks suffer respiratory problems, nausea, dizziness, and disorientation from exposure to these chemicals. Others are severely mutilated or even killed when flammable chemicals in the labs catch fire or explode.

The sales of cold and allergy medicines that contain ephedrine and pseudoephedrine, important meth ingredients, are now carefully tracked and controlled by pharmacies.

Restricting Access to Meth Ingredients

The proliferation of cheap, simple meth labs means that targeting users alone won't stop the spread of the drug. Instead, recent legislation has been designed to make it more difficult to produce methamphetamine. Because most of the ingredients used in the manufacture of meth are technically legal, there is no way to stop people from acquiring them. However, laws have been passed that make it difficult for people to obtain large amounts of these substances.

The Comprehensive Methamphetamine Control Act (MCA) of 1996 placed restrictions on the purchase of chemicals used to make meth. It also increased the maximum legal penalties for manufacturing the drug. In 2000, the Methamphetamine Anti-Proliferation Act (MAPA) was passed as part of the Children's Health Act of 2000. Once again, it increased penalties for the possession or sale of meth. It also created a budget for training law enforcement officers to investigate methamphetamine manufacturing and seize meth labs.

A number of states have passed laws restricting the amount of ephedrine or pseudoephedrine that a person can purchase. Oregon has been particularly aggressive in this regard. In April 2005, the state required people to sign a registry when buying over-the-counter cold medicines containing ephedrine or pseudoephedrine. This way, the police know who has been buying products containing ephedrine or pseudoephedrine and how much that person has been buying. This law forces potential meth cooks to travel across the state border if they want to get meth-making supplies. The law has substantially reduced the state's illegal meth activity. In 2004, Oregon law enforcement agents seized 447 meth labs. In 2005, after the law went into effect, they seized only 185 labs.

Since 1989, five federal laws and dozens of state laws have been passed that are designed to halt the production of meth. The most recent federal law was the Combat Methamphetamine Epidemic Act of 2005. This law restricts the amount of ephedrine and pseudoephedrine that can be purchased within a specific time period (about 300 pills a month) and provides regulations for how these products must be stored by pharmacies in order to prevent theft.

Though it is hard to argue with the these federal and state laws' effectiveness, they have not entirely stopped meth production. In Oregon, for example, some meth cooks travel out of state to buy ephedrine or pseudoephedrine, or a number of

An Oklahoma Bureau of Narcotics spokesperson poses with the readily available ingredients and simple equipment needed to make a "shake-and-bake" batch of meth.

meth cooks hop from pharmacy to pharmacy and purchase the maximum amount of ephedrine or pseudoephedrine they can without being recorded on the registry. This practice is known as "smurfing" and allows meth cooks to operate in a somewhat limited manner despite restrictions. While meth is still prevalent in Oregon, it is now much more difficult to manufacture there.

In response to restricted access to ephedrine and pseudo-ephedrine, a new, simpler form of production has emerged, one that requires far less of those two ingredients to make a small batch of meth. Instead of a sophisticated and hidden lab, meth producers are increasingly using a two-liter soda bottle, just a few cold pills, and household chemicals. The pills are crushed and combined in the bottle with the chemicals. The mixture is shaken, and the end result is a small batch of meth. Meth producers are now making these batches on-the-go—in their cars or in bathroom stalls. Though the mixture is not heated and no open flames are involved, potentially deadly accidents are still as common as they were when meth was being made in labs. If the soda bottle contains any oxygen, a powerful explosion can result if the pressure grows too great during the so-called "shaking and baking." In addition, after the residual powder is removed from the bottle (to be smoked, snorted, or injected by the drug abuser), the soda bottle remains toxic. Thousands of these toxic bottles are being discarded along roadways, creating an environmental and public health danger.

Federal Antimeth Legislation

After the terrorist attacks of September 11, 2001, the U.S. Congress passed the Patriot Act. The goal of the Patriot Act was to make it easier for intelligence agencies and law enforcement agents to prevent terrorist attacks on American soil. The Patriot Act was a controversial piece of legislation: many people feel it restricts people's civil liberties to an unacceptable degree.

A number of additional provisions were added to the Patriot Act, including a package of antimethamphetamine measures in 2005. This package of legislation, called the Combat Methamphetamine Epidemic Act, was the most aggressive meth bill ever put in front of Congress. This legislation requires states to place medicines with ephedrine or pseudoephedrine behind pharmacy counters. It also limits the amount of medicine containing ephedrine or pseudoephedrine a person can purchase and forces people to sign a logbook so their purchases can be tracked. Many large retail chains such as Wal-Mart and Walgreens had already chosen to limit the sale of cold products, but this new legislation made such restrictions mandatory.

The Combat Methamphetamine Epidemic Act placed further restrictions on the sale of meth ingredients and gave the police additional tools in the fight against the drug. It also allocated extra money to help meth addicts get help recovering from their addiction.

6

METH USE
AND
CRIMINAL BEHAVIOR

Not only is producing and selling meth a crime, using meth is also a crime in and of itself. Yet just being on meth also increases the likelihood that a person will commit a secondary crime. The link between drugs and crime is consistently established by data collected in various drug abuse and criminal justice studies. One such study found that 42.5 percent of male arrestees in Anchorage, Alaska, tested positive for drug use, while nearly 78 percent tested positive in Philadelphia, Pennsylvania. The

Avoiding Prison Time

Introduced in Florida in 1989, drug court is a system in which drug offenders can enter treatment to avoid a prison sentence. Not everyone is considered for drug court. Offenders who are guilty of less serious crimes, such as driving under the influence or drug possession, rather than of serious or violent crimes, are more likely to be eligible. People who participate in drug court have to plead guilty and enter treatment. They also have to pass regular drug tests. If they successfully complete treatment, the charges against them are dropped. If they don't, however, they go to prison. There are now drug courts in every U.S. state.

statistics were more wide-ranging for women: about 33 percent of women arrested in Laredo, Texas, tested positive for drugs, while more than 80 percent of women arrested in New York City tested positive for drugs. The crimes most closely associated with people who test positive for drugs are vehicular theft, breaking and entering, and other forms of robbery, as well as prostitution and drug sales.

Stealing Someone's Identity

Identity theft is the illegal acquisition of a victim's personal information, such as a Social Security number or credit card information. This crime has become increasingly common among meth addicts. While people steal a victim's personal information for a number of purposes, one of the most

A criminal bent on identity theft searches through trash for discarded credit card bills, phone bills, medical records, and other personal identifying information.

common is credit card fraud. By taking out a fake credit card in someone else's name, a criminal can quickly purchase any number of things and then simply throw the card away before the fraud is detected and the card is seized or cancelled.

Some meth addicts turn to identity theft to fund their habit. Often, they steal people's mail and give it to the head of an identity theft ring in exchange for drugs. With the increased energy, concentration, and wakefulness that meth affords its users, people can spend all night stealing mail from mailboxes or even going through people's trash, looking for things such as preapproved credit card applications.

Meth Trafficking and Possession

The Controlled Substances Act (CSA), which is part of the Comprehensive Drug Abuse Prevention and Control Act of

1970, classifies all drugs into one of five categories, known as schedules. This 1970 act is the foundation upon which all drug laws in the United States passed since 1970 have rested. The U.S. Drug Enforcement Administration (DEA) sorts drugs into schedules based on their beneficial value for use in medicine, the potential harm they can cause, and how addictive they are.

Methamphetamine is a schedule II drug. Schedule II drugs are used for medicinal purposes but also have a high potential for abuse and addiction. Other schedule II drugs include cocaine, opium, morphine, and barbiturates. The penalties for trafficking (selling on a large scale) schedule II drugs are very stiff and always involve prison time. If a person is caught trafficking 0.2 to 1.7 ounces (5 to 49 grams) of pure methamphetamine, or 1.8 to 17.6 ounces (50 to 499 g) of mixed methamphetamine, he or she faces a prison sentence of five to forty years and a fine of up to $2 million. Multiple offenses carry even stricter sentences.

Penalties for possession of schedule II drugs vary by state and region and may include jail sentences or assignment to a drug rehabilitation clinic. Federal penalties might include a one-year prison sentence and a fine for first-time offenders. The penalties are steeper for multiple offenders. Many states have passed even stricter sentencing laws for people who assist in the manufacture of methamphetamine.

CHAPTER 7

THE HIGH COST OF METH PRODUCTION, USE AND ADDICTION

Meth has a tremendous impact on individuals, families, and entire communities. Once meth has its hooks in a user, it doesn't want to let go. It can take years for a meth user to recover fully from using the drug. During this time, the person may feel fuzzy-headed and unsatisfied with life because the brain's centers of pleasure and reward have been altered and damaged by the drug. Once meth gets a foothold in a community, it can be economically and socially devastating.

Meth's Primary Victims: Family and Loved Ones

The side effects of meth use can include paranoia and extreme aggression. Often, the targets of aggression are the people closest to the users. In some areas of California where meth is particularly prevalent, the majority of domestic violence cases that police investigate involve meth use.

A woman who is crashing after a five-day meth and painkiller binge cannot rouse herself to respond to the cries of her three-year-old nephew. The boy's father is serving a long prison term for meth-related crimes.

The children of meth addicts are often abused and neglected. There are countless stories of law enforcement agents raiding someone's home containing a meth lab and finding children living in extremely squalid conditions. The process of cooking meth can leave highly toxic residue on surfaces all over the home, constantly exposing all occupants of the house to the drug. Chemicals that need to be kept cold are often stored in the refrigerator, where they can contaminate food. Often, the children who live in meth labs are extremely malnourished.

The Cost of Combating Meth

Cleaning up meth labs, providing law enforcement agents with training, imprisoning dealers, providing treatment for meth addicts, and putting the children of some meth addicts into protective services all cost money. The annual cost of funding enforcement of meth laws nationwide is more than $4 billion, while drug treatment and rehabilitation for meth addicts costs more than $500 million a year. The total annual costs of meth use nationwide—factoring in crime, law enforcement, lost productivity, health care, treatment, and foster care expenses—has been estimated at more than $23 billion. This works out to more than $26,000 a year for each person who has used meth in the past 12 months, and more than $73,000 a year for each meth addict. Some of this money can be recovered through fining meth lab operators. However, the taxpayers end up bearing the bulk of the burden.

Fetal Damage

Just like any other harmful substance, meth can have a profound effect on unborn children. However, there is not enough data for researchers to come to any solid conclusions about the effects of meth on children in the womb. Still, anecdotal evidence has revealed some startling facts. Some babies are born prematurely to mothers who are using meth. Even those who are carried to full term exhibit a number of the same behaviors and symptoms as premature babies. For instance, they may have trouble swallowing and are often very sensitive to touch.

Although none of the children studied appeared to be mentally disabled when they grew older, there is a chance that unborn children may suffer strokes while in the womb. Meth constricts blood vessels in a user's body, and when a pregnant woman uses the drug, it can also constrict the blood vessels of the placenta, the organ that nourishes an unborn baby. This can affect the fetus's heart rate and its growth. Although some deformities and physical abnormalities have been observed in fetuses exposed to methamphetamine, there has not been any definitive evidence linking the two.

Targeting Small Labs

One reason that meth users and producers have successfully resisted the efforts of drug enforcement agents is that the drug is so easy to manufacture. A person's garage, trailer, or even a rented storage space can serve as a meth lab. When a meth lab is busted by the police, another one can easily spring up in its place.

There is no surefire way for drug enforcement agents to determine the location of a meth lab. There are some clues that homes may contain labs, such as extensive security around the house, large amounts of trash outside, and unusual chemical odors coming from inside. Another sign that a home may contain a meth lab is that its occupants always go outside when smoking cigarettes, sometimes standing a good distance away from their home so as not to ignite the flammable chemicals inside the laboratory.

Superlabs produce most of the United States' meth and are thus a bigger priority for law enforcement. However, small meth labs account for many more fires and explosions, and therefore present their own challenges and dangers to the community. People who operate small, clandestine labs are not as well organized as large drug cartels. Generally, the cooks at small meth labs aren't highly skilled, and it's common for them to be on drugs while manufacturing the meth. This can seriously impair their judgment, leading to accidents and fires.

Raiding Meth Labs

When meth labs are raided, drug enforcement agents wear respirators and hazardous materials (hazmat) suits as they

The volatile, explosive, and environmentally toxic waste products of meth production must be handled and disposed of with enormous care and safety, as this hazmat team member does at the site of a raided meth lab in North Little Rock, Arkansas.

confiscate the illegal materials inside. For each pound (0.5 kilograms) of meth a lab produces, it also produces about 5 to 7 pounds (2.3 to 3.2 kg) of toxic waste. This waste is extremely dangerous, and there is no legal way for a person running a meth lab to dispose of it.

As a result, the toxic waste from meth production is often poured down storm drains or into rivers, or it's just dumped on the ground. These chemicals are major pollutants and are often flammable, explosive, and corrosive. They are hazardous to the health of not only the person dumping them but to people in the community near where they are being made. The waste left over from cooking a batch of meth can easily leak into the groundwater, sometimes harming people who don't even live near the lab.

If the meth lab is still in operation at the time of a raid, it first must be "neutralized" by police. The police subdue and arrest anyone on the premises and make sure that there is no danger of the meth lab exploding. After the lab has been neutralized, any clearly toxic chemicals are safely disposed of. The chemicals remaining in the lab are then tested to determine how dangerous they are. It costs law enforcement officers up to $10,000 to clean up a small-scale meth lab. A superlab can cost over $150,000 to clean. More than 10,000 meth labs are seized in the United States every year, and the federal Drug Enforcement Administration (DEA) spends almost $20 million a year cleaning up meth labs.

8

KICKING THE
HABIT
AND
GETTING CLEAN

I f you are addicted to meth, there are people and organizations out there that can help you break the addiction. A supportive network of friends and family members can make the difference between life and death for you. The emotional support of loved ones often helps addicts acknowledge their problems and encourages them to find the strength to stop using drugs.

Rehabilitation facilities across the United States offer treatment for various types of drug addiction. Some patients

An antidrug billboard provides a graphic warning about the physical ravages of meth use.

voluntarily enter drug rehab. Others are ordered to undergo treatment by an employer, school, or court of law. Many drug treatment centers offer family programs. They provide a place where family members can have safe, counselor-mediated discussions with the person seeking treatment. These programs also help family members begin to build a new, drug-free life in partnership with their loved ones. There are specialized clinics that deal specifically with meth addiction or ones in which all the residents are teenagers.

Recognizing the Problem and Breaking the Cycle

There is still a lot that researchers don't know about meth's long-term effects on the body and brain. The medical community offers no cure-all drug to free meth addicts from their disease. Unlike heroin or cocaine, meth withdrawal does not involve many physical symptoms. The psychological effects of meth withdrawal, however, can be devastating. Antidepressants can be helpful in getting meth users through the tough period after they stop using the drug, but they are not a cure for addiction.

After a thorough detoxification, treatment for methamphetamine use generally involves therapy to help users recognize their problem and break the patterns of their addiction. Drug addicts are generally used to a way of life that centers around the drug they abuse. The sooner a person recognizes that he or she has a drug problem and seeks treatment for it, the easier quitting will be. The more advanced a drug problem is, the more difficult it is to overcome. With the help of friends and family members and a supportive environment, however, meth users can get their lives back together.

Reaching Out

It is estimated that approximately 10.4 million Americans aged twelve or older have used methamphetamines at least once in their lives. The number of people being admitted to treatment for amphetamine and methamphetamine abuse and addiction more than doubled during the first decade of the twenty-first century. Almost one in ten drug-related admissions to emergency rooms involves methamphetamines, and about 15,000 people die each year due to stimulant abuse.

Although a person may think that he or she is fine, someone who uses meth needs help. There are a few ways to tell if someone you know has been using meth. People who are high on meth often talk very rapidly and compulsively perform some sort of repetitive action. They may also have dilated pupils and complain of an irregular heartbeat. Other common side effects are nausea, diarrhea, chest pains, and shortness of breath. Users may have scabs on their arms or face from picking at their skin. They may also have needle marks on their arms if they inject the drug. Over time, users often begin neglecting personal hygiene and may appear unwashed. Someone on meth may also be extremely paranoid, aggressive, or even violent.

If you know that a person is using meth, the addiction will worsen unless he or she gets treated for addiction. Before a person can help another person, however, the addict needs to want to be helped. The first step in ending addiction is to admit that a problem exists. Try to help a friend or family member see how meth has changed his or her life, the stranglehold it has on it, and the gravity of the problem. When your loved one sees and admits that there is a problem, then you can help him or her end the cravings by finding a treatment plan that works.

TEN

1. I use meth on occasion, about once a month. Does this mean I am addicted?

2. Can meth be used in moderation?

3. What are some signs that someone is overdosing on meth?

4. Since I have stopped taking meth, I feel depressed. How long will this feeling last? Will I ever feel happy again?

5. If I enter a drug rehab facility, will I face charges for having done meth?

6. Should I have my parents go to therapy with me?

7. What are the legal risks of carrying meth?

8. What can I do to get rid of my meth scars and fix my broken teeth?

9. I think someone is operating a meth lab in our neighborhood. Whom should I contact to investigate this? Can I give an anonymous tip?

10. What is the best way for me to stay off meth for good?

GLOSSARY

amphetamine A stimulant drug first synthesized in the nineteenth century.

Benzedrine One of the first commercially released forms of amphetamine. Benzedrine was intended to be used as a decongestant and came in an inhaler. In 1970, amphetamine became illegal in the United States, spurred partly by Benzedrine abuse.

black market An underground (not officially sanctioned) marketplace where illegal goods are sold and purchased.

cocaine An illegal stimulant with effects some-what resembling those of methamphetamine.

detoxification Detoxification, or detox, is a span of time in which a person is monitored while abstaining from drug use. Detox lasts until all traces of the drug leave the user's body.

dopamine An important natural chemical that, among other things, causes a person to feel pleasure, enjoyment, and satisfaction.

euphoria An intense feeling of pleasure.

hepatitis C A disease that attacks the liver.

human immunodeficiency virus (HIV) A virus that destroys the immune system and that causes acquired immunodeficiency syndrome (AIDS).

insomnia The inability to sleep.

meth mouth The extensive tooth decay most meth users experience.

paranoia A psychological condition in which a person believes that people are out to harm him or her.

tolerance A body's resistance to a drug's effects.

tweaking When a meth user desperately tries to achieve the same rush that he or she experienced when first doing the drug, but without any success.

withdrawal The often unpleasant, and sometimes deadly, physical symptoms that drug addicts experience after abstaining from particular drugs.

FOR MORE INFORMATION

Families Anonymous, Inc.
P.O. Box 3475
Culver City, CA 90231-3475
(800) 736-9805
Web site: http://www.familiesanonymous.org
Families Anonymous is an organization dedicated
to helping the family members of an addict. There
are a number of Families Anonymous meetings all
over the United States.

Narcotics Anonymous
World Service Office
P.O. Box 9999
Van Nuys, CA 91409
(818) 773-9999
Web site: http://www.na.org
Narcotics Anonymous is a community-based
nonprofit association of recovering drug addicts
in more than 116 countries. Membership is open
to all drug addicts who seek help.

The National Clearinghouse for Alcohol and
Drug Information
1 Chokecherry Road
Rockville, MD 20857
(877) SAMHSA-7 (726-4727)

Web site: http://www.ncadi.samhsa.gov
The Clearinghouse for Alcohol and Drug Information, sponsored by the U.S. Department of Health and Human Services, contains a wealth of information about drugs and alcohol.

Public Health Agency of Canada
130 Colonnade Road
A.L. 6501H
Ottawa, ON K1A 0K9
Canada
Web site: http://www.phac-aspc.gc.ca
PHAC's primary goal is to strengthen Canada's capacity to protect and improve the health of Canadians and to help reduce pressures on the health care system.

Web Sites

Due to the changing nature of Internet links, Rosen Publishing has developed an online list of Web sites related to the subject of this book. This site is updated regularly. Please use this link to access this list:

http://www.rosenlinks.com/dac/meth

FOR FURTHER READING

Adamec, Christine. *Amphetamines and Methamphetamine* (Understanding Drugs). New York, NY: Chelsea House, 2011.

Berne, Emma Carlson. *Methamphetamine* (Compact Research). San Diego, CA: Referencepoint Press, 2007.

Brady, Betty. *Meth Survivor: Jennifer's Story and How One Community Fought Back.* Bloomington, IN: Authorhouse, 2006.

Braswell, Sterling R. *American Meth: A History of the Methamphetamine Epidemic in America.* Lincoln, NE: iUniverse, 2006.

Erdmann, Larry R. *Methamphetamine: The Drug of Death.* Lincoln, NE: iUniverse, 2006.

Etingoff, Kim. *Methamphetamine: Unsafe Speed* (Illicit Drugs). Broomall, PA: Mason Crest Publishers, 2007.

Harrow, Jeremy. *Crystal Meth* (Incredibly Disgusting Drugs). New York, NY: Rosen Central, 2007.

Johnson, Dirk. *Meth: America's Home-Cooked Menace.* Center City, MN: Hazelden Publishing, 2005.

Landau, Elaine. *Meth: America's Drug Epidemic.* Minneapolis, MN: Twenty-First Century Books, 2008.

Lee, Steven J. *Overcoming Crystal Meth Addiction: An Essential Guide to Getting Clean.* New York, NY: Da Capo Press, 2006.

Marcovitz, Hal. *Methamphetamine.* San Diego, CA: Lucent Books, 2005.

Mehling, Randi. *Methamphetamine* (Drugs: The Straight Facts). New York, NY: Chelsea House, 2007.

Owen, Frank. *No Speed Limit: The Highs and Lows of Meth.* New York, NY: St. Martin's Press, 2008.

Reding, Nick. *Methland: The Death and Life of an American Small Town.* New York, NY: Bloomsbury, 2010.

Sheff, Nic. *Tweak: Growing Up on Methamphetamines.* New York, NY: Atheneum, 2009.

Taylor, Nicolas T., and Herbert C. Covey. *Helping People Addicted to Methamphetamine: A Creative New Approach for Families and Communities.* Westport, CT: Praeger Publishers, 2008.

Weisheit, Ralph, and William White. *Methamphetamine: Its History, Pharmacology, and Treatment.* Center City, MN: Hazelden Publishing, 2009.

INDEX

About the Authors

Lara Norquist is a writer who lives in Minneapolis, Minnesota.

Frank Spalding has written numerous books about substance abuse, crime, and teen mental health wellness. He lives in Brooklyn, New York.

Photo Credits

Cover, p. 1, chapter openers DEA; pp. 4–5 iStockphoto/Thinkstock; p. 10 PhotoQuest/Getty Images; p. 12 © Mark Allen Johnson/ZUMA Press; p. 14 Hemera/Thinkstock; p. 17 Digital Vision/Thinkstock; pp. 19, 28–29, 37 © AP Images; p. 22 © Robin Nelson/ZUMA Press; p. 27 © Fairbanks Daily News-Miner/ZUMAPRESS.com; pp. 33, 49 © Robert King/ZUMA Press; p. 35 Craig Mitchelldyer/Getty Images; p. 42 © Zoriah/ZUMA Press; p. 45 Jonathan Torgovnik/Getty Images; p. 52 © Michael Siluk/The Image Works.

Photo Researcher: Amy Feinberg